This book is due for return on or before

10/04
29 OCT 2007
07 APR 2008
10 JUL 2009

**Chase Terrace
Technology College**
03181

Keeping Unusual Pets

SNAKES

Sonia Hernandez-Divers

Heinemann LIBRARY

www.heinemann.co.uk/library
Visit our website to find out more information about Heinemann Library books.

To order:
☎ Phone 44 (0) 1865 888066
📄 Send a fax to 44 (0) 1865 314091
💻 Visit the Heinemann Bookshop at www.heinemann.co.uk/library to browse our catalogue and order online.

First published in Great Britain by Heinemann Library, Halley Court, Jordan Hill, Oxford OX2 8EJ a division of Reed Educational and Professional Publishing Ltd. Heinemann is a registered trademark of Reed Educational and Professional Publishing Ltd.

OXFORD MELBOURNE AUCKLAND JOHANNESBURG BLANTYRE
GABORONE IBADAN PORTSMOUTH (NH) USA CHICAGO

© Reed Educational and Professional Publishing Ltd 2002
First published in paperback 2003
The moral right of the proprietor has been asserted.

All rights reserved. No part of this publication may be reproduced, stored in a retrieval system, or transmitted in any form or by any means, electronic, mechanical, photocopying, recording, or otherwise without either the prior written permission of the Publishers or a licence permitting restricted copying in the United Kingdom issued by the Copyright Licensing Agency Ltd, 90 Tottenham Court Road, London W1P 0LP.

Designed by Celia Floyd
Originated by Dot Gradation Limited
Printed by Wing King Tong in Hong Kong/China

ISBN 0 431 12406 X (hardback)
06 05 04 03 02
10 9 8 7 6 5 4 3 2 1

ISBN 0 431 12410 8 (paperback)
07 06 05 04 03
10 9 8 7 6 5 4 3 2 1

British Library Cataloguing in Publication Data

Hernandez-Divers, Sonia M.
 Snakes. – (Keeping unusual pets)
 1. Snakes as pets – Juvenile literature
 I. Title
 639.3'96

Acknowledgements
The Publishers would like to thank the following for permission to reproduce photographs: Ardea: p. 19 (top); Ardea/Douglas Napier: p. 28 (bottom); Ardea/Geoff Trinder: p. 10 (top); Bruce Coleman Collection: p. 12 (bottom); Bruce Coleman Collection/John Cancalosi: p. 4; Heather Angel: p. 6; Maria Joannou: p. 41 (bottom); Natural Visions/Brian Rogers: p. 9 (top); NHPA/Daniel Heuclin: pp. 11 (top), 9 (bottom); NHPA/James Carmichael Jr: p. 11 (bottom); NHPA/Martin Wendler: p. 5 (top); Oxford Scientific Films/David M. Dennis: p. 7 (top); Oxford Scientific Films/John Mitchell: p. 7(bottom); Oxford Scientific Films/Mike Price: p. 16; Science Photo Library: p. 10 (bottom); Science Photo Library/Tom McHugh: p. 5 (bottom); Trevor Clifford: p. 45; Tudor Photography: pp. 8, 12 (top), 13, 14, 15 (top), 15 (bottom), 17 (top), 17 (bottom), 18, 19 (bottom), 20, 21 (top), 21 (bottom), 22 (top), 22 (bottom), 23 (top), 23 (bottom), 24, 25, 26, 27, 28 (top), 29, 30, 31 (top), 31 (bottom), 32, 33, 34 (top), 34 (bottom), 35, 36 (top), 36 (bottom), 37 (top), 37 (bottom), 38 (top), 38 (bottom), 39, 40, 41 (top), 42, 43 (all pics), 44

Cover photograph reproduced with permission of NHPA/Daniel Heuclin

Every effort has been made to contact copyright holders of any material reproduced in this book. Any omissions will be rectified in subsequent printings if notice is given to the Publishers.

Disclaimer
All the Internet addresses (URLs) given in this book were valid at the time of going to press. However, due to the dynamic nature of the Internet, some addresses may have changed, or sites may have changed or ceased to exist since publication. While the author and Publishers regret any inconvenience this may cause readers, no responsibility for any such changes can be accepted by either the author or the Publishers.

No animals were harmed during the process of taking photographs for this series.

Contents

What is a snake? 4
Snake facts 6
Is a snake for you? 12
Choosing your snake 14
What do I need? 20
Looking after your snake 24
Feeding your snake 28
Handling your snake 32
Some health problems 36
Keeping a record 42
Finding out more 44
Glossary 46
Useful addresses 47
More books to read 47
Index 48

> Any words appearing in the text in bold, **like this**, are explained in the Glossary.

What is a snake?

Snakes belong to the **reptile** family. Reptiles have no hair and their bodies are covered with scales. They do not make milk for their young and they are **cold-blooded**, which means they need to soak up heat from their surroundings. There are three types of reptiles: lizards, turtles and snakes.

Snakes are long, legless creatures that slither along the ground. They do not have eyelids or external ears. They **shed** all their skin in one piece at regular intervals.

Squeezing to death

Some snakes kill their **prey** by squeezing it. This is called **constriction**. They grab an animal firmly and then wrap their muscular bodies around it, squeezing the animal so it cannot breathe. Eventually, the animal **suffocates**. Once the animal is dead, the snake swallows it whole.

Some snakes have small pits above their lips. These pits are heat-sensing organs that allow the snakes to sense the warm bodies of their prey.

Did you know?

- All snakes are **carnivorous**, which means they eat other animals.
- Snakes eat large amounts of food at once, and one large meal can take them weeks to digest!
- Some snakes eat fish, while others eat insects, birds, other snakes, eggs or **rodents**.
- Some **species** of snake can unhinge their jaws so that they can swallow very large animals.

Beware of poison!

About one third of the world's snakes are **venomous**. Venomous snakes have hollow **fangs** on their upper jaw and **venom glands** – small **organs** at the base of the fangs – that make a powerful poison. When the snake bites its prey, **venom** is injected into it. The snake simply waits for the venom to work, before swallowing the dead animal.

Need to know
- Snakes are protected by law – which means you are not allowed to catch snakes from the wild.
- Children are not allowed to buy pets themselves. In any case you should always have an adult with you when you buy your pet.
- Most countries have laws that say that pets must be treated with respect. It is your responsibility to make sure that your snake is healthy and well cared for. Always take your pet to the vet if it is ill or injured.

This is a type of snake called an anaconda. Anacondas kill their prey by wrapping themselves around the animal and squeezing it tightly until it can no longer breathe.

The fangs of a venomous snake are normally folded up inside its mouth, but when the snake prepares to bite, its fangs unfold. The snake sinks its fangs into the prey and injects venom into the animal's body.

Snake facts

It is useful to know how snakes live and hunt in the wild, because this will help you to understand your own pet snake.

Did you know?

There are over 2500 **species** of snakes in the world. Like most **reptiles**, they live in the warmer parts of our planet. But snakes can be found in a variety of **habitats**. The bamboo viper lives in the bamboo thickets of China, the dwarf adder lives in the dry, powdery sand deserts of southwest Africa, and the yellow-bellied sea snake spends most of its life floating in the currents of the Pacific Ocean.

Grass snakes are very common in the UK. If you are lucky, you might get a glimpse of one **basking** in the sunshine!

In the UK, the most common snake is the grass snake. Grass snakes eat frogs and small fish and can usually be found close to streams and ponds.

Australia has 140 species of land snakes and 30 species of sea snakes. About 100 Australian snakes are poisonous, but only 12 are likely to inflict a wound that could kill you. There are many Australian snakes that are harmless to humans. These include the carpet snake or common python, patterned with black and brown. Another is the diamondback snake, greenish-black with yellow diamond-shaped markings. The largest is the rock python, which can be up to 7 metres long.

Not so scary

Unfortunately, snakes have suffered from a bad reputation. People used to be very afraid of them and killed any snake they met. It is true that some snakes are poisonous and should be avoided, but, in general, we now recognize that snakes are beautiful, useful members of the animal kingdom. Without snakes, the world might be swarming with rats and mice!

Garter snakes like this one are very common in the USA and can even be found in towns and cities, where they hunt for small insects and fish.

Snakes in danger

Many species of snake are **endangered** and are likely to become **extinct**. This is because their homes are being destroyed to make room for farmland, roads or houses. Snakes are also in danger of dying out because people have been killing them for hundreds of years. For this reason, many countries now have laws that prohibit killing snakes or collecting them from the wild.

Many snakes hunt rats and mice, and help to keep their numbers down.

Tasting the air

Snakes have a very good sense of smell, but they do not have noses like we do. A snake flicks out its tongue and picks up little invisible **particles** that are floating in the air. When it brings its tongue back into its mouth, it presses it against a special **organ** on the roof of its mouth (called the vomeronasal organ) that detects the 'smell' of the particles that the tongue has picked up! So, you could say that a snake 'tastes' the air in order to smell it!

> This snake is picking up particles from the air on its tongue. In order to 'smell' the air, it needs to press its tongue against a special organ inside its mouth.

Hearing and feeling

Snakes do not have external ears, but because they can feel vibrations they are not completely deaf. For example, if you walk next to a snake, the vibrations that your feet make on the ground are enough for a snake to 'hear' you coming.

Even though its scales seem thick, a snake's skin is very sensitive. Snakes can sense very slight temperature changes through their skin. They can also feel when they brush against even the softest things.

Snakes' eyes

Most snakes do not have very good eyesight. In fact, you can probably see better than most snakes! They also do not have eyelids. Instead, they have clear scales that cover their eyes. These scales keep their eyes moist and protect them.

Unlike many snakes, blue racers use their eyes to help them find their **prey**. They travel through grass with their heads above the blades looking out for animals.

Snake sounds

Most of the time, snakes are silent, but they can make some interesting noises.
- Snakes hiss when they are frightened or angry. They do this by forcing air out through their mouth very fast.
- Some snakes have a 'rattle' on their tail. It is made from a special group of scales that rub together and make a loud noise when the snake vibrates its tail.

The rattlesnake shakes its rattle to warn **predators** to keep away.

9

Hiding and running

Snakes have a lot of enemies. Hawks, owls, fish, foxes, skunks, racoons, badgers and many other animals all eat snakes. So a snake has to be very careful not to be seen or captured.

Most snakes use their colouring as **camouflage** to help them hide. The pattern on a snake's skin usually matches the background of the place where it lives. When a **predator** approaches, most snakes choose to stay still and blend in with their surroundings until the danger has passed.

Snakes have many enemies in the wild, so they have to stay well hidden or fight back fiercely.

If they are discovered, snakes have to run! A wild snake that hears a strange noise or sees a large animal approaching will slither away fast. That is why if you go walking in the countryside, all you will ever see of a snake is a flash of movement!

Some snakes are incredibly well camouflaged. Can you find the snake in this picture?

10

Fighting back

Snakes will defend themselves in several different ways if they are grabbed by a predator:

- Some snakes have **scent glands** that produce a foul smell. This is meant to convince the predator that the snake would not make a suitable meal!
- Some snakes try to squeeze the animal that grabs them, by wrapping their bodies around a leg, for example.
- Some snakes bite, using their sharp, needle-like teeth. Most small snakes only make little pinprick holes when they bite, but large snakes, such as pythons, can strike with force and cause severe wounds.
- Some snakes are **venomous** and sink their **fangs** into their attackers and inject them with poison. This is very painful and the **venom** of some snakes can kill even quite large animals.

Many venomous snakes use their colouring to scare off predators. For example, the coral snake, which is highly poisonous, has very noticeable coloured bands on its body. These warn predators to stay away. Other snakes have colours similar to venomous snakes, even though they are not poisonous at all. This type of self-defence is called mimicking.

The venomous coral snake has bands of bright colours that warn predators to stay away.

Milk snakes are not venomous but some of them have the same bands of colours as the venomous coral snake. That way predators *think* they are poisonous and avoid eating them.

11

Is a snake for you?

Some **species** of snakes can make fascinating, interesting pets, but before you buy one, you should think about some of the plus and minus points of keeping snakes.

The right snake

Only a few species of snake make truly good pets. Others, such as pythons, should not be handled unless you have an experienced adult with you. Some snakes – especially poisonous ones – are *very* dangerous and should not be kept in **captivity**, except by professional snake keepers.

The ideal pet snake should not be poisonous and should not get too big for its owner to be able to look after it. Some snakes, such as boa constrictors, can grow up to 3 metres long and need several people to handle them.

Snakes can be very friendly and inquisitive! Your pet snake will soon seem like a friend.

As well as growing very large, pythons tend to be moody and can strike out and bite their owners. They are not good pets for beginners!

Snake good points

- Snakes are beautiful.
- Many snakes are gentle.
- They are very quiet pets.
- They are easy to keep clean.
- They are easy to feed.
- They are fascinating to watch.

Snake not-so-good points

- Snakes need to be kept warm and dry.
- You will need to buy some specialized equipment.
- Snakes have to be fed on frozen rats or mice.
- Snakes can escape easily, and hide anywhere.
- Some species can bite very hard.
- Some snakes are poisonous – and these should not be kept as pets.

Snakes feed on dead mice or rats, which can put some people off keeping snakes as pets.

Yes or no?

If you think you are ready to keep a snake, great! But remember, being responsible for a living thing can be a lot of work. Most snakes tend to be long-lived – even a small corn snake will live for ten years – so you will be looking after your pet for a long time. Snakes need special care to stay healthy and happy. You will need to do some homework to understand the needs of your pet.

Choosing your snake

Snakes that have been born in **captivity** make the best pets. Wild snakes are very nervous and are more likely to develop diseases. They also tend not to eat very well as pets.

There are many different types of snake available from pet shops or snake breeders. If you have never owned a pet snake before, it is best to start with a snake that is small, gentle and easy to look after. Two good examples are the corn snake and the black rat snake.

Corn snakes

Corn snakes come from the eastern part of the USA. They live in pine forests, on rocky hillsides and in farming areas. Corn snakes are most active at night or in the early morning and late evening. They are mainly ground-dwellers, which means it is rare to find them in trees.

Young corn snakes eat small lizards, little frogs or insects, such as crickets. As they get bigger, they hunt larger animals, such as rodents.

This is a typical corn snake. It has an arrowhead pattern on the top of its head and a golden coloured body with reddish-brown markings.

Did you know?

The scientific name for a corn snake is *Elaphe guttata*. The first word is Latin for 'deerskin', because these snakes have soft skin that looks like the hide of a deer. The second word means speckled or spotted, and refers to the markings on their body.

Corn snake colours

Wild corn snakes are covered in red or brown blotches. But in captivity, corn snakes have been bred to be lots of different colours – so you might find one that is completely white, or mostly red or one that has a wide variety of patterns!

The pattern on this corn snake's belly looks like piano keys!

Great pets!

Corn snakes make great pets because:
- They are not very expensive.
- They do not get very big – they only grow to around 1 metre long.
- They can live for as long as 20 to 25 years.
- They are gentle.
- They eat well.
- They do not have many special needs.

The biggest problem with corn snakes is that they are real escape artists! Once they have got out of their tanks, they can easily hide!

Reptile breeders have bred many different colours of corn snakes. This **albino** corn snake has hardly any colouring at all.

Rat snakes

How do you think the rat snake got its name? Correct! It eats rats. In the wild, rat snakes eat rats, mice, voles, squirrels and birds. Young rat snakes eat frogs, lizards and young mice.

Rat snakes originally come from the USA. They live in heavily wooded areas, but they have also become used to living around people, so they can often be found in barns or in gardens too. They also spend a lot of time in trees. In most areas of the USA, it is **illegal** to collect wild rat snakes or hurt them in any way because they are **endangered**. The most common rat snake is the black rat snake.

Did you know?

The scientific name for a rat snake is *Elaphe obsoleta obsoleta*. It shares its first name with the corn snake and they are, in fact, related. Indeed, they are cousins! Some people call corn snakes the red rat snake.

In the wild, rat snakes can have a varied diet of rats, mice, voles, squirrels and birds.

Noisy tail

The black rat snake has some special scales on its tail that make a rattle-like sound to scare off **predators**. It deliberately imitates rattlesnakes so other animals will leave it alone. But it is *not* related to rattlesnakes and is not **venomous**.

Black rat colours

The black rat snake is a slender, shiny snake. When they are young, black rat snakes have a pattern of dark grey or black blotches and spots over a mostly light grey body. As they get older, they turn mostly black, but can have some grey or brown colour. Reptile breeders have produced different coloured varieties, such as the white-sided black rat snake.

This black rat snake is black on top, white on its underside and has an 'eye line' across each eye.

What's the difference?

What makes black rat snakes different from corn snakes?
- They are more active during the day.
- They are excellent climbers.
- They **hibernate** in the winter.
- They can grow up to 2 metres long!
- They can live up to fifteen years in captivity.
- They vibrate their tail when they are scared.

Black rat snakes make excellent pets because they get used to people very easily.

17

Buying your pet snake

Corn snakes and rat snakes should always be bought from a pet shop or a reptile breeder. Reptile breeders often advertise in newspapers, on the Internet and in reptile magazines.

Reptile breeders keep and **breed reptiles** such as snakes and lizards. They can be very helpful because they have lots of experience of looking after snakes. A reptile breeder can give you information on how to care for your snake, where to get snake food, what equipment you will need and how to keep your snake healthy. A reptile breeder will also show you how to check your snake for common problems.

Reptile magazines have fascinating articles about snakes, as well as advertisements for reptile breeders and food suppliers.

Top tips

A good reptile breeder will help you choose which snake is best for you.
- You will probably want a snake that looks beautiful, but remember to check if it is also **alert** and active.
- Look at its skin and scales – they should look bright and shiny.
- Ideally, you should buy a young snake, so it can get used to you from an early age.

Warning signs
Do not buy a snake that:
- seems sleepy or is not very active when you hold it
- is not flicking its tongue
- has cuts or scrapes on its body
- has dull skin
- has **mites** or **ticks** on its body.

Important questions
Before you buy a pet, you will need to know some basic details about your snake and how to take care of it. Here are some questions to ask the reptile breeder or pet shop owner:
- Was the snake **bred** in captivity? You should not buy snakes that have been taken from the wild.
- How old is it? It is best to buy a young snake.
- What is it eating? You will need to buy the same food.
- How often is it eating? This will help you plan meals.
- How much is the snake eating at one time? This will help you decide how much to feed it.
- How often is it **shedding** its skin? You will want to make sure that your snake is shedding regularly (see page 37).

This snake has ticks clinging onto its head, between its scales.

Corn snakes are curious and inquisitive. An alert snake will flick its tongue often and move around the tank.

19

What do I need?

Your new pet will need a comfortable place to live. Corn snakes and black rat snakes can be kept in tanks, like the ones used for fish. When your snake is young and small a 20-litre or 40-litre tank will be big enough. But as time passes, your snake will grow and need a bigger tank (about 80 to 100 litres). You should always make sure that the tank or enclosure you get for your snake has several openings, so that the air is always fresh inside.

Keep it in!

Your snake will spend a great deal of time and effort trying to get out of its tank, so your tank will need a tight-fitting lid! Make sure your tank has a lid that snaps closed or a sliding door that has a lock on it. Never underestimate the strength of your snake. Snakes are bundles of muscle and will push the lids open if they do not fit very tightly!

The tank should be at least as long as your snake, but ideally twice as long. It should also be wide enough for your snake to turn around comfortably.

Substrate

Susbstrate is the material you will put on the bottom of the tank. It will give your snake something soft and warm to lie on.

- Natural materials like topsoil can be used, but they are difficult to keep clean.
- Pine wood shavings make good substrate because it is easy to remove any soiled shavings.
- You can also use paper towels, newspaper or artificial grass for your substrate. They do not look as attractive as wood shavings and will not feel as natural to your snake, but they are very easy to replace.

You can cover your snake's tank with shavings or torn-up paper towels. It is best to put your snake in a container without shavings when you feed it. That way, the wet **prey** will not get covered in little pieces of shavings.

Water bowl

Choose a water bowl that is heavy enough to stop your snake from tipping it over. Black rat snakes like to soak in their bowls, so the bowl should also be big and deep enough for them to climb into it.

Most snakes love to have a good long soak in their water bowl!

Safety first!

Never use cedar wood shavings as substrate. The fumes from this type of wood can be harmful to your snake.

Shelter

It is very important to give your snake a place to rest! Your pet will like a little plastic house that you can make yourself, or a pile of natural items such as branches and rocks. You should give your pet a shelter in both the warm and the cooler areas of its tank (see page 27 to find out about tank temperatures).

Cage furniture

Putting rocks and branches in your pet's tank will imitate the snake's **environment** in the wild. Remember, snakes spend a lot of time climbing on and in between rocks and fallen logs to search for their **prey**. You can put a branch inside the tank so your snake can climb onto it. More importantly, snakes need a hard object, such as a rock, to rub against and get rid of their old skin.

Making a home for your snake is an easy project. Cut a small hole in the side of a medium-sized plastic tub. Put it upside down and you have a snake house!

This corn snake has just shed its skin. Your snake will need things to rub against to help it lose its old skin.

22

You could also try adding some plants to the tank to make your snake feel more at home. But first check with an adult – some plants are poisonous to snakes.

Snake plants or fig plants are a good choice for your snake's tank. They look attractive and have very tough leaves.

All change!

Every once in a while, change all the furniture in your snake's home. This will not confuse your snake – it will just make it feel as if it has moved to a new place! You will notice your snake will flick its tongue and try to re-explore its 'new' home. This is good exercise for your pet and will keep it from getting bored.

Replacing all the furniture in your snake's home will keep your snake happy and is a lot cheaper than buying a new tank.

Looking after your snake

Looking after a snake is a big responsibility. There are lots of things you will need to do on a regular basis.

Keeping things clean

Your snake's tank will need to be cleaned thoroughly every two weeks. Keeping your snake's home clean is the best way to make sure it stays healthy and happy!

Take all the contents out of the tank and clean them individually. The tank can be cleaned with warm water and soap. Instead of soap you can use a household disinfectant that is marked on the bottle as safe for babies. After using disinfectant, rinse the tank thoroughly with lots of water and then let it dry completely before you put back any of its contents or your snake.

Keep your snake in a separate container while you clean its tank. It can watch you from a safe spot!

Top tip

It is a good idea to have a small, plastic container with holes in it where you can put your snake while you clean its home. That way it will not escape and you will not hurt it with any cleaning materials you are using.

When cleaning the tank, you must make sure that the disinfectant you use is not harmful to snakes.

When to clean

- Every day, change the water in your snake's water bowl so that the water is always fresh.
- Every two days, remove any **faeces** or soiled **substrate** from the tank.
- Every two weeks, clean the entire tank and all its contents.

Home from home

Try to create a home that is as close as possible to that which your snake would experience in the wild. In the wild, a snake would wake up and go to a sunny spot to absorb heat through its skin – this is called **basking**. When it had absorbed enough heat, it would begin to be active and move about. If it got too hot, it would move to a shady area or slither inside a burrow to cool down.

Your snake will want to do the same things in its tank. You will need to set up a **heat source** at one end of your snake's tank so that your pet has one very warm area for basking. It will also need a cooler area in the centre of the tank where it can be active, while the far end of the tank should be even cooler still so your snake can cool down. Use a thermometer to check the temperature in the different parts of the tank. If the temperature drops lower than 23°C in any part of the tank, your snake might not want to eat and could get sick.

Safety first

Never use heaters that look like artificial rocks. Although some people recommend these 'hot rocks' as a heat source for reptiles, your snake can get burnt!

Many people think that heating pads are the best method of heating your tank. They do not give out any light and your snake should not get burned.

Not too bright

Snakes like it to be dark for at least 12 hours a day. Make sure your heat source does not produce a lot of light and remember to turn off bright lights at night so your snake can sleep!

Which heat source?

There are several ways to heat your snake's home.

- You could use a heating light bulb. This is a powerful electric light bulb that gives out lots of warmth. However, you must make sure that the light is not too bright.
- You may prefer to use a ceramic bulb. Ceramic bulbs make a lot of heat, but they do not make light. They are a great way to keep a tank warm without having to have a light turned on all the time.
- You may choose to use heating pads or heating tape. These can be put under the tank to heat it from the bottom.

Ask your reptile breeder for advice on which would be the best heat source for you. Whichever method you choose, always make sure that your snake does not have direct access to the heat sources you use.

The temperature at the heated end of the tank (pictured) should be around 32°C. The temperature in the middle of the tank should be around 26°C, while the temperature at the far end should be about 24°C. Unlike in this picture, you should always cover your heat pad with lots of woodchips, so your snake cannot get burned.

Feeding your snake

All snakes are **carnivorous**, which means that they eat other live animals. Both corn snakes and rat snakes eat a variety of live animals in the wild. When they are young they eat some insects, frogs, small lizards, **rodents** and even eggs!

Dinnertime

Snakes are fun to feed! Since corn snakes and rat snakes are mainly **nocturnal** (more active at night), it is a good idea to feed them either late in the evening or early in the morning. You will enjoy watching your snake smell, grab and swallow its food – it is a fascinating sight!

Snakes can unhinge their jaws to swallow surprisingly large objects.

Young snakes enjoy eating crickets. You can buy containers of crickets like these from a pet shop or reptile breeder.

Top tip

It is best not to feed your snake with live food. If your snake does not eat the live animals as soon as they are offered, they might bite your pet and injure it severely. Also, just think how frightening it is for a live mouse to be stuck in a tank with a snake! It is actually **illegal** in some countries to feed live **prey** to snakes!

If your snake is young when you get it, you can offer it crickets and very small frozen mice. You can get these from a pet shop or a reptile breeder. The frozen prey will have to be defrosted first. Talk to an adult about the best way to defrost these animals. Snakes normally eat warm, live animals so you may want to warm them up by soaking them in warm water. Do *not* use a microwave to defrost frozen prey. It will become cooked and will not be very good for your snake.

Growing well?

A baby snake should grow pretty fast. If it is shedding its skin every three to four weeks, it is probably growing at a good pace. It is a good idea to measure and weigh your snake every week or so. You will need a simple weighing scale and a measuring tape.

Try to weigh and measure your young snake regularly to make sure it is growing steadily. But do not use your kitchen scale to weigh your snake, as snakes can leave behind bacteria that are dangerous to people.

How often? How much?

Snakes take a very long time to digest their food so they do not need to be fed very often.

- Very young snakes should be offered food once a week. They can be fed one small newborn mouse or several crickets (between five and ten).
- **Juvenile** snakes (snakes that are less than one year old) can be fed every seven to ten days. One large mouse is about right.
- Adult snakes should be fed once every two to three weeks. They will eat two large mice or one medium rat at each mealtime.

Check with your reptile keeper or pet shop to see how much you should feed your snake. As your snake grows, it may eat less and not as often.

Sometimes you can persuade your snake that its food is alive by moving it around.

Encouraging your snake

Your snake will probably eat the food you give it. But you might need to encourage it to eat. Ask an adult to help you open up the mouse or rat so your snake can smell it better. You could also try using tongs or something similar to make the **prey** 'move' a little in the tank. Your snake might think it is alive and be more likely to eat it!

Top tip

Do not use your fingers to hold the prey as you move it. Your snake might not be able to tell the difference between the prey and your fingers, and could bite you!

A little variety

Feeding pre-frozen rodents to your snake will provide it with a balanced, **nutritious** meal, but your snake will appreciate some variety. Other things that can be fed to your snake include frozen chicks and quail eggs. The chicks should be one to two days old. Your snake will eat two or three quail eggs at a time.

Big bulge?

After your snake has swallowed its prey, you might notice a bulge in its body. This bulge should not be too big. If it is very large, your snake might be having trouble digesting its food. Next time, feed your snake less food.

Never use your hand to put your snake's food in the tank. That way, your snake will not confuse your hand with its food – which could lead to accidents!

This snake has just eaten a meal. Can you see the bulge inside its body?

Top tip

It will take several days for your snake to digest its food. To digest their food well, snakes need to be warm and quiet. It is best not to play with your snake for at least two to three days after you have fed it. It needs to rest to digest!

Handling your snake

Snakes may look slimy and hard, but actually they are very soft and dry! Snakes are wonderful to touch and hold, but imagine how big you must seem to a young snake. Do not be surprised if when you try to pick up your snake the first few times, it seems frightened and tries to slither away. This is normal. In the wild, a snake has lots of enemies – mostly larger animals and birds trying to eat it. Its main defence is to slither away as fast as it can and hide.

Slowly does it

- It is best to let your snake get used to the idea of having your hand in its tank before you try to touch it. Move your hand around very gently until your snake realizes that your hand is not going to hurt it.
- When your snake is used to your hand in its tank, you can slowly start to touch your pet. First try just stroking your snake with one finger. When it seems used to that, try picking it up slowly.

With a little patience, you can train your snake to get used to your hand in its tank. Do not make any loud noises and move very slowly.

Snake-proofing your room

Before you pick up your snake, take a good look around. If your pet gets away while you are holding it, where will it go? Spend a few minutes 'snake-proofing' your room before you take it out to play!

- Remove any sharp objects that could injure your snake.
- Make sure there are no holes or spaces that your snake could slip into and then be impossible to find or rescue!

Picking up your snake

The best way to pick up a snake is to scoop it up gently. Use one hand to hold it gently behind the head and the other hand to support the rest of its body. *Never* hold your snake with just one hand. It is best to hold your snake over a surface, like a bed or table, in case it wriggles free!

Your snake will feel much more secure if you hold it close to your body. You will also be less likely to drop it!

Snakes are curious

Snakes are very curious, so your pet's first instinct will be to crawl in and out of your fingers, around your arms and maybe even inside your shirt sleeves! It is quite surprising to feel the muscles of the snake moving on your arm!

It might feel a little strange to have a snake inside your shirt, but do not worry – it will not hurt you!

Escape artist!

If your snake tries to get away, gently pick it up by its body and bring it back to your hands. But if your snake is constantly trying to get away, it is time to put it back in its tank! It is probably still a little nervous of being touched and needs a rest in order to calm down.

If your snake keeps trying to get away from you, put it back in its tank and let it have a rest!

Getting to know you

You might also notice that your snake is flicking its tongue a lot when you hold it. This is its way of smelling you and recognizing you! If you handle your snake regularly, it will get used to you. After a few weeks, it will calmly sit on your hands.

If your snake bites...

If your snake is not used to you or if something frightens it, it might get scared and bite you. Do not panic! Corn snakes and rat snakes are unlikely to hurt you – their teeth are very small! If your snake does bite you, you might find it does not want to let go. That is normal. Do not try to pull its mouth away from your hand, but support the snake with your other hand and tell an adult straightaway. The adult will help you to remove the snake. Wash your tiny cuts thoroughly and apply some antiseptic ointment. Your parents or guardians may take you to a doctor.

Snake teeth are loose and are designed to come off when they are biting their **prey**, so you might find some snake teeth are left behind! Do not worry about this, your snake will grow some new teeth soon.

Do not worry if your snake flicks its tongue out a lot – it is just getting to know you!

Safety first

Even a healthy, clean snake can have **bacteria** on its body that could make you sick. To avoid any danger of spreading bacteria, follow these simple rules:

- Wash your hands with warm water and soap every time you finish handling your snake.
- Do not eat or drink while you are playing with your snake.
- Do not let your snake slither across places where you put food, such as kitchen counters.

Some health problems

Whenever you take your snake out of its tank, check it carefully. It should have a filled-out, rounded body without any wrinkles and it should look **alert** and active. If your snake is slow and sluggish it may just be too cold. Check your thermometer to make sure that the tank is warm enough.

If you are not sure how to read a thermometer, ask an adult to help you. It is important to get it right.

Corn snakes and rat snakes are usually healthy, but they sometimes develop a few health problems. The next few pages describe some problems that your pet might experience.

When snakes get too cold they become very still and take no interest in their surroundings.

Not drinking

Most reptiles can survive for days or even weeks without food, but they cannot survive without water. Make sure your snake has clean, fresh water every day. You can encourage your snake to drink by soaking it in a shallow warm water bath for a few minutes.

Not eating

There are many reasons why your snake might not eat. It might be too cold, or too ill, or it might not like the food you are offering it. Sometimes snakes get tired of eating the same thing all the time. Try a different food and see if your pet starts to eat again.

If your snake is still not eating, even after you have changed its diet, pick it up and check if it seems ill. If you are worried, tell an adult. You may need to take it to the vet.

If you are worried about your snake, it never hurts to ask an adult for a second opinion.

Shedding problems

If you notice that your snake is not shedding its skin well – if parts of its old skin are stuck to it or it is not shedding in one piece – then it might need some help. Gently soak your snake in a warm water bath. Make sure it has a rock or a branch in its tank that it can rub against to help get the old skin off. If there is still skin hanging onto parts of your snake's body, talk to an adult about taking your snake to the vet.

Sometimes a warm bath can help your snake to finish shedding normally. You can see that this snake is shedding because its eyes are covered with old, milky-looking skin.

Vomiting

If you find that your snake is vomiting the food you feed it, you might be feeding it too much at once. Next time, give it less or feed it two smaller animals instead of one large one. If the problem continues, tell an adult.

38

Danger signs

Look out for the following warning signs. They could mean that your snake is seriously ill.

- Is your snake not interested in food, even after you have changed its diet?
- Does your snake seem less active than usual, even when the temperature in its tank is warm enough?
- Does it not respond to your hand or touch like it used to?
- Does its skin look saggy and wrinkly, and does it keep its eyes closed a lot?
- Does it look skinny?
- Does it have any lumps or bumps on its skin?
- Has part or all of your snake's skin turned a different colour?

Checking your snake regularly is the best way to make sure that any problems are spotted as early as possible.

Visiting the vet

Just as you went to a doctor for check-ups when you were a baby, your snake will also need to visit a vet for a physical examination. Soon after you buy your snake, ask an adult to make an appointment with a vet who is used to working with **reptiles**. This will give your vet a chance to meet your snake. The vet will also be able to give you useful advice on how to care for your pet and how to recognize when it might be ill.

Checking your pet

Your vet will want to give your snake a thorough physical examination. During the examination the vet will probably:
- weigh your snake
- watch your snake from a distance to make sure it is active and lively
- look for **mites** and other skin **parasites**
- make sure the snake is not too skinny
- open the snake's mouth and look at its teeth and gums
- feel the snake's body to make sure its **organs** are normal
- listen to its heart and lungs
- check a sample of your snakes' **faeces** to make sure they do not contain parasites.

Soon after you get your pet, take it to the vet for a check-up.

The vet will give your snake a thorough physical examination.

Saying goodbye

Corn snakes and rat snakes can live as long as ten to fifteen years, but however well you care for your pet, one day it will die. Sometimes a snake will die peacefully and unexpectedly. This will come as a shock for you, but do not blame yourself. There is probably nothing you could have done.

As a caring owner, it is hard to know when to let your pet be put to sleep to save it from suffering. Your snake may be very old and in pain or it may have a serious illness. Your vet will give your snake a small injection. This does not hurt your pet, it just makes it sleepy. Soon your snake will be asleep and its heart will have stopped beating.

Feeling upset

You will feel upset when your snake dies, especially if it has been a friend for many years. It is perfectly normal for people to be sad when a pet dies. It can help to have a special burial place and maybe to plant a flower or a shrub on it. Eventually, the pain will pass and you will be left with happy memories of your pet.

Keeping a record

It is fun to keep a record of your pet snake. Buy a big scrapbook and fill it with notes and photos. Then you can look back at it and remind yourself of all the things you and your pet have done together. Your snake scrapbook can also include general information about snakes and how to care for them.

You will soon build up a very useful record of your pet, but remember to put the fun things in too!

A special scrapbook

There are many things you can write in your scrapbook.
- Describe your trip to the pet shop or reptile breeder to buy your snake. What did your snake look like and how did you feel about it?
- Write down the name you chose for your pet.
- Note down special events in the life of your snake, such as the first time it shed its skin.
- Make a note of all the cool things your snake does, such as winding its way inside your shirt!

Top tip
You can cut out articles and pictures of snakes from magazines and stick them in your scrapbook.

Black rat snake

Corn snake

Add labels to the pictures after you have stuck them in. Otherwise you might forget what they are!

Take pictures of your snake every few months and put them in your snake scrapbook. It will be fascinating to look back later and see how your snake has grown.

Important information
Your scrapbook is a very good place to keep important information. Write down the phone number of your vet, your local reptile breeder and the company where you buy your snake's food. Because you do not need to feed your snake very often, it is a good idea to note down when you last fed your snake and how much it ate. It is also helpful to keep a record of your snake's weight each time you weigh it. That way you can see if it is growing steadily. Similarly, write down when your snake sheds its skin so you can make sure that it is shedding regularly.

Finding out more

It was not long ago that most people hated snakes. They thought that snakes were dirty or evil. We now know that these things are not true. Snakes are just like any other animal. They breathe, need food and feel fear just like other animals. But they are also unusual and fascinating creatures. Keeping a snake of your own will make you want to find out more about snakes and the way they live.

Sharing the fun

There are many people who love snakes as much as you do! Ask a reptile breeder or at your pet shop if they know of a snake club in your local area that you could join. Getting together with other people who appreciate snakes can be fun. They can tell you about their experiences and you can share your stories too.

It is fun to get together with other snake owners and compare your experiences.

Now try this

Here are some more ways to find out about snakes:
- Visit your local library and bookshop – there are hundreds of books written on snakes.
- Go to zoos and nature centres – they will have fascinating snakes to see and lots of information on snakes in the wild.
- With an adult, visit other snake lovers' websites and the websites of reptile breeders. You will see beautiful pictures of many types of snake and read about their unusual lives.
- Go to a magazine shop and find out what magazines they have on snakes or **reptiles**. A good magazine will contain lots of useful information.

Most zoos have a reptile house with a wide range of interesting snakes – some of the snakes in zoos are incredibly dangerous!

Glossary

albino animal or person with very light or white skin, fur or hair
alert always watchful and paying attention
bacteria tiny one-celled creatures that can cause disease
bask to lie in the sun and absorb its warmth
breed to mate and produce young
camouflage colours and markings to help blend in with surroundings
captivity under the control of humans
carnivorous meat-eating
cold-blooded animal having the same body temperature as the surrounding air or water
constriction coiling around prey in order to strangle it
endangered at risk of being completely wiped out
environment surroundings and weather conditions in an area
extinct when all individuals of a species are no longer living
faeces solid waste matter (poo) passed out of the body, also called droppings
fang long, pointed tooth
habitat place where an animal or plant lives or grows
heat source place where warmth or heat comes from, such as the Sun
hibernate to sleep or hide away during the cold time of year
illegal against the law
juvenile young or immature animal
mite small blood-sucking insect
nocturnal animal that is active at night

nutritious food source that provides the energy needed by an animal
organ part of the body that has a specific purpose
parasite small creature, such as a tick or worm, that lives on or in another animal
particle very small piece of something
predator animal that lives by killing and eating other animals
prey animal killed by another animal for food
reptile cold-blooded animal with scaly or tough skin
rodent member of the animal family that includes rats, mice and voles
scent gland special place on some animals where they produce a smelly substance that can be spread around to mark their territory
shed to lose a covering, such as a snake shedding its skin
species a group of animals that is similar and can produce young
substrate soft material put in the bottom of a snake tank
suffocate to stop breathing. This leads to death.
tick small creature that lives on another animal's skin and sucks its blood
venom poison made by some animals to inject into their enemies or prey
venom gland the place on an animal where the venom is produced
venomous animal that attacks its prey or enemies using venom

Useful addresses

British Herpetological Society
c/o Zoological Society of London
Regent's Park
London NW1 4RY
United Kingdom
http://www.thebhs.org/

Association for the Study of Reptilia and Amphibia
Cotswold Wildlife Park
Burford
Oxfordshire OX8 4JW
United Kingdom

The Australian Reptile Park
Pacific Highway
Somersby
NSW 2250
Australia
http://www.reptilepark.com.au

More books to read

There are not many books about snakes written for young readers, but the ones below should be enjoyed by snake owners of all ages.

Corn and Red Rat Snakes, Jerry G. Walls (TFH Publications, 1996)

Corn Snakes, R. D. Bartlett (Barron's Educational Series, 2000)

Keeping and Breeding Snakes, Chris Mattison (Cassell Illustrated, 1998)

Rat Snakes, Jerry G. Walls (TFH Publications, 1994)

Your First Snake, Elizabeth Walker (Kingdom Books, 2000)

Index

anacondas   51

baby snakes   29, 30
bacteria   29, 35
basking   6, 26
bites   11, 13, 30, 35
buying a snake   5, 14, 18–19

camouflage   10
captivity, snakes bred in   14, 15, 19
carnivorous animals   4, 28
cold-blooded animals   4
constriction   4, 5, 11
coral snakes   6, 11,
corn snakes   13, 14–15, 18, 19, 22, 28, 35, 36, 41
crickets   28, 29, 30

death   41
digestion   30, 31

endangered species   6, 7, 16
escaping   15, 20, 33
eyes   9

faeces   25, 40
fangs   5, 11
food   4, 6, 7, 13, 14, 16, 19, 28–29, 30–1, 37, 38, 43
frozen food   13, 29, 31

grass snakes   6

handling your snake   32–4
health problems   36–40
hearing   8
heat-sensing organs   4
heat source   26, 27
heating pads   26, 27
hibernation   17
hissing   9
'hot rocks'   26

juvenile snakes   30

legal facts   5, 7, 16, 29
lifespan   13, 15, 17, 41
live prey   29

mice and rats   13, 29, 30
milk snakes   11
mimicking   11
mites and ticks   19, 40

nocturnal animals   28
noises   9

parasites   19, 40
plants   23
poisonous snakes   5, 6, 7, 11, 12, 13
predators   9, 10, 11, 16, 32
prey   4, 7, 9, 14, 16
pythons   6, 11, 12

rat snakes   16–17, 18, 21, 28, 35, 36, 41
rattlesnakes   6, 9, 16
reptile breeders   18, 19, 45
reptiles   4, 6, 37, 40

scales   4, 8, 9, 16
scent glands   11
scrapbook   42–3
self-defence   11, 16
shelter   22
skin   8, 10, 19, 39
skin shedding   4, 19, 22, 29, 38, 43
smell, sense of   8
snake-proofing a room   33
species of snake   6
substrate   21, 25

tank cleaning   24–5
tank furniture   22–3
tanks   20–3, 26
teeth   11, 35, 40
temperature conrol   26, 27, 36
tongue flicking   8, 19, 23, 34, 35

venom   5, 11
vets   37, 40, 41
vomiting   38

water   37
water bowl   21, 25
weight   29, 40, 43
wild snakes   6–11, 14, 16, 19, 26, 32
wood shavings   21, 27